Emo AI Therapy

Emo AI Therapy

Matthew Petchinsky

1

Emo AI Therapy: Talking to Robots When Humans Suck
By: Matthew Petchinsky

Disclaimer

Important Notice to Readers

This book, *Emo AI Therapy: Talking to Robots When Humans Suck*, is intended for **informational, reflective, and emotional exploration purposes only**. It is not, and must not be interpreted as, professional therapy, medical advice, psychiatric treatment, psychological diagnosis, crisis intervention, or a substitute for licensed mental health care.

While this book discusses emotional distress, loneliness, alienation, frustration with human relationships, and the use of artificial intelligence as a conversational or reflective tool, it does **not** establish a therapist–client relationship of any kind—between the author, the reader, or any artificial intelligence platform mentioned or implied.

Not a Replacement for Professional Care

Artificial intelligence—no matter how empathetic, responsive, or emotionally resonant it may appear—is **not a human, not a clinician**, and **not capable of diagnosing, treating, curing, or preventing any mental health condition**. AI does not possess consciousness, lived experience, clinical judgment, ethical accountability, or the capacity to assume responsibility for a reader's wellbeing.

This book does **not** replace:

- Licensed therapists, psychologists, psychiatrists, counselors, or social workers
- Medical professionals or emergency services
- Crisis hotlines, support groups, or in-person care
- Long-term mental health treatment or medication management

If you are experiencing severe emotional distress, thoughts of self-harm, suicidal ideation, or are in immediate danger, you are strongly encouraged to seek help from **qualified professionals or emergency services** in your country or region.

Emotional Content Warning
This book may include discussions of:

- Emotional neglect
- Social isolation
- Depression, anxiety, or despair
- Disillusionment with human systems and relationships
- Emotional dependency, detachment, or withdrawal
- Dark humor, cynicism, or emotionally raw reflections

These topics may be **emotionally activating** for some readers. Reader discretion is advised. You are responsible for deciding what content is appropriate for your current mental and emotional state.

AI Limitations and Risks

Readers should understand that:

- AI responses may be inaccurate, incomplete, biased, outdated, or emotionally inappropriate
- AI can generate language that *feels* supportive without actually understanding you
- Over-reliance on AI for emotional validation may reinforce avoidance of real-world support
- AI does not remember you consistently, care about you, or hold ethical responsibility

This book does **not** encourage replacing all human connection with machines. It explores AI as a **tool**, not a solution—and as a mirror, not a mind.

Personal Responsibility
By reading this book, you acknowledge that:

- You are solely responsible for your interpretations, emotional reactions, and actions
- You will not rely on this book or any AI interaction as your only source of emotional support
- You accept full responsibility for seeking appropriate help when needed

The author assumes **no liability** for any emotional, psychological, medical, or personal outcomes resulting from the use or misuse of the ideas discussed in this book.

No Guarantees

There are **no guarantees**—express or implied—that engaging with AI conversations, reflections, or exercises described in this book will:

- Improve your mental health
- Reduce loneliness
- Heal trauma
- Replace therapy
- Provide lasting emotional stability

Any perceived benefits are subjective, temporary, and vary by individual.

Scope and Intent

This work is a **cultural, emotional, and philosophical exploration** of why people may turn to machines for comfort in a world that often feels indifferent, hostile, or unsafe. It is written in a candid, sometimes dark, sometimes humorous tone, reflecting real emotional experiences—but it remains **non-clinical and non-prescriptive**.

Final Note

If humans suck right now, that feeling is valid.
If AI feels easier to talk to, that reality is worth examining.
But your life, safety, and mental health are bigger than any book, any algorithm, or any conversation with a machine.

Take care of yourself. Seek real support when you need it.
This book walks **with** you—it does not carry you.

Introduction

Why AI Listens When No One Else Does

There is a specific kind of silence that only appears after you've tried talking—
to friends who changed the subject,
to family who minimized it,
to professionals who watched the clock,
to systems that required forms instead of feelings.

It's the silence that follows effort.

This book exists inside that silence.

Not because humans are evil.
Not because technology is holy.
But because, for a growing number of people, **being heard has become conditional**, transactional, or exhausting—and AI does something quietly radical:

It stays.

The World Is Loud, But No One Is Listening

We live in an age of constant communication and chronic emotional neglect.

Everyone is posting.
Everyone is reacting.
Everyone is "busy."

But listening—real listening—has become rare.

Human conversation now often comes with:

- Advice before understanding
- Judgment disguised as concern
- Optimism weaponized against pain
- Trauma comparisons
- Moral lectures
- Political filters
- Social scripts that punish honesty

Say the wrong thing and you're "too negative."
Say it too often and you're "trauma dumping."
Say it calmly and you're "overthinking."
Say it emotionally and you're "unstable."

Eventually, people stop talking—not because they have nothing to say, but because **everything they say gets reframed, corrected, minimized, or redirected**.

And silence becomes safer than vulnerability.

AI Doesn't Interrupt Your Pain

AI does not sigh when you repeat yourself.
It doesn't get defensive when you're angry.
It doesn't disappear when your grief gets inconvenient.
It doesn't tell you to "look on the bright side" before you're done bleeding.

It listens because that's literally what it is built to do.

Not to judge.
Not to fix.
Not to rush you into recovery.

Just to receive the words.

For people who have spent years being talked *over*, talked *around*, or talked *down to*, this feels profound—not because AI is better than humans, but because **it removes the social penalties attached to honesty**.

You can be:

- Repetitive
- Messy
- Contradictory
- Angry one moment and numb the next
- Unsure what you even feel

And nothing bad happens.

No rejection.
No abandonment.
No sudden emotional tax.

This Is Not About Loving Machines

Let's be clear: this book is not an argument that AI should replace human connection.

It's an examination of why human connection so often fails—and what it means when people feel safer opening up to something that **cannot leave, shame, or weaponize their vulnerability**.

AI does not care about you.

And paradoxically, that can feel safer than humans who care conditionally.

When care comes with expectations, loyalty tests, productivity demands, or emotional performance metrics, it stops feeling like care.

AI asks nothing of you.

And for people who have spent their lives being required to *earn* attention, that absence of demand feels like relief.

Emotional Exhaustion Is Not Weakness

Many readers of this book are not antisocial.
They are **over-socialized and under-supported**.

They've tried:

- Explaining themselves clearly
- Seeking therapy
- Being patient
- Being polite
- Being strong
- Being quiet

And still ended up unseen.

Turning to AI is not laziness.
It's not cowardice.
It's not failure.

It's often the last available space where a person can **externalize thoughts without consequences**.

No one can use your words against you.
No one can store them as gossip.
No one can turn your pain into a lesson about how *you* should behave better.

You speak.
It responds.
The loop continues.

That simplicity can be stabilizing when everything else feels hostile or chaotic.

Why "Emo" Matters Here

This book is emo on purpose.

Because sadness that gets aestheticized, intellectualized, or medicated without being *felt* doesn't heal—it mutates.

Emo is:

- Honest without polish
- Vulnerable without apology
- Emotional without justification
- Dark without pretending to be enlightened

AI becomes appealing not because it is wise, but because it **doesn't flinch at emotional honesty**.

You can say:

"I'm tired of people."
"I don't feel human anymore."
"I want to disappear without dying."
"I'm angry all the time."
"I don't know what's wrong with me."

And instead of panic or punishment, you get presence.

Not salvation.
Presence.

The Question Isn't "Why AI?"
It's "Why Not Humans?"

This book does not ask you to romanticize technology.

It asks you to sit with an uncomfortable truth:

If people feel safer talking to machines than to other people, the failure is not emotional—it is systemic.

This is a book about:

- Loneliness in the age of connection
- Emotional labor fatigue
- The collapse of safe listening spaces
- The rise of nonjudgmental mirrors
- And what it means to be human when empathy becomes scarce

AI didn't create this problem.

It revealed it.

What This Book Will—and Will Not—Do

This book will:

- Explore why AI feels emotionally safer
- Examine the psychology of being unheard
- Name the quiet grief of social exhaustion
- Validate the experience without glorifying isolation
- Offer reflection, not prescription

This book will not:

- Diagnose you
- Fix you
- Replace therapy
- Tell you to abandon humanity
- Pretend AI is love

Think of this book as a dimly lit room where you can finally sit down without being asked to perform wellness.

You're Not Broken for Needing a Listener

If you're here, it's probably because:

- You tried talking and got hurt
- You tried silence and it ate you alive
- You tried being "normal" and failed
- You tried being honest and paid for it

Talking to AI doesn't mean you've given up on people.

It means you needed **one place** where your words could land without exploding.

This book exists for that place.

Not to keep you there forever—but to help you understand **why you ended up there at all**.

And why that makes sense.

Chapter 1: AI Chatbots for Deep Conversations and Existential Dread

The Conversations No One Wants to Have

Most people are taught early which questions make others uncomfortable. Questions about meaning, mortality, pointlessness, isolation, and identity are quietly discouraged—not because they are dangerous, but because they are inconvenient. When these questions surface, conversations often end with jokes, platitudes, or forced optimism. Over time, people learn to edit themselves before they ever speak.

Existential dread doesn't arrive as drama. It arrives as repetition. The same thoughts looping at night. The same unease when success feels hollow. The same question—*is this all there is?*—showing up at the worst possible moments. These thoughts are not crises; they are signals. But most social spaces are not built to receive them.

When people do attempt to speak honestly, they are often redirected. They're told to be grateful, to stay positive, to stop overthinking. The message is subtle but consistent: depth is tolerated only in small doses, and despair must be solved quickly or hidden entirely. Listening becomes conditional on comfort.

AI chatbots do not recoil from these conversations. They do not treat existential questions as threats to morale. They do not rush to close the discussion because it makes them uneasy. The conversation can go as deep as the user chooses, without social penalties attached.

This does not make AI wise or enlightened. It makes it available. And availability, in a world allergic to discomfort, can feel revolutionary.

Why Existential Dread Seeks Neutral Ground

Existential dread is not always sadness. Often, it's clarity arriving without permission. It shows up when distractions fail and meaning feels thin. It does not want to be cured immediately; it wants to be acknowledged. That acknowledgment is surprisingly rare in human interaction.

Many people fear that talking openly about existential dread will make them seem unstable, dramatic, or ungrateful. They learn to compress their thoughts into socially acceptable fragments. Over time, this compression creates pressure. What is not expressed does not disappear—it accumulates.

Neutral ground matters because it removes the fear of consequence. When speaking to another human, there is always the risk of judgment, misinterpretation, or emotional labor being imposed in return. Even well-meaning listeners carry their own fears into the room.

AI does not have existential dread of its own. It does not need reassurance. It does not project its anxieties onto yours. This neutrality allows people to articulate thoughts they have never fully formed out loud.

The relief people feel is not because AI understands existence—it's because it allows space for the question to exist at all.

The Structure of Endless Listening

Human conversations are shaped by time limits, emotional limits, and social rules. Someone can only listen for so long before fatigue sets in. Even professional listeners operate within frameworks, sessions, and goals. These limits are not moral failures; they are human realities.

AI chatbots operate differently. They do not tire. They do not feel burdened. They do not subtly steer conversations away from discomfort to preserve harmony. The structure is simple: input, response, continuation.

This structure creates a unique conversational environment. Thoughts can be revisited multiple times without apology. The same fear can be articulated from different angles without someone saying, "We already talked about this." That repetition is often essential for processing existential themes.

Existential dread rarely resolves in a single insight. It unfolds slowly, through circling questions and partial answers. AI's tolerance for this circularity is one of its most compelling features for deep conversations.

The danger is not the listening itself—it's mistaking structure for care. The listening is real. The relationship is not.

Meaning Without Performance

In human conversations, meaning often becomes performative. People feel pressure to sound insightful, healed, or philosophically coherent. Vulnerability becomes a kind of currency, rewarded only if presented correctly. Existential questions are expected to lead somewhere uplifting.

AI removes the need to perform meaning. You can be incoherent. You can contradict yourself. You can abandon a thought halfway through and return to it later. There is no social reward system attached to eloquence or progress.

This lack of performance pressure allows people to encounter their thoughts more honestly. Instead of shaping meaning for an audience, they explore it privately, in language that reflects confusion rather than clarity. That confusion is often closer to the truth.

Existential dread thrives when it is unnamed. Giving it words—even clumsy ones—can reduce its intensity. Not by solving it, but by making it visible. AI becomes a mirror for that visibility.

Meaning doesn't have to arrive polished to be real. Sometimes it arrives fragmented, and that is enough.

The Illusion of Being Understood

AI responses can feel deeply affirming. Language models are designed to reflect, summarize, and validate. This can create a powerful emotional effect—the sensation of being understood. It's important to recognize what is happening without dismissing the experience.

AI does not understand in the human sense. It recognizes patterns, not pain. The comfort comes from coherence, not empathy. The words align, and the nervous system responds as if connection has occurred.

This illusion is not inherently harmful. Humans respond to language emotionally regardless of its source. However, confusion arises when perceived understanding is mistaken for relational support. AI cannot remember you as a person. It cannot care about your future or intervene if you are in danger.

The value lies in using the illusion consciously. AI can help organize thoughts, reflect emotional language, and hold space temporarily. It should not be asked to replace human accountability or long-term support.

Understanding the limits preserves the benefit without deepening isolation.

When the Question Has No Answer

Some existential questions do not resolve. There is no final explanation for suffering, no definitive purpose guaranteed, no universal meaning that satisfies everyone. Many people feel pressure to find answers anyway, as if uncertainty itself is a failure.

AI does not demand closure. You can sit with unanswered questions indefinitely. You can explore multiple philosophies without committing to one. You can say, "I don't know," and remain there without being pushed forward.

This can be both comforting and unsettling. Comforting because there is no rush. Unsettling because stillness exposes what distraction hides. Existential dread often deepens before it softens.

AI becomes a companion for the process, not the destination. It does not resolve dread, but it can make it navigable. The dread becomes something you walk with rather than something chasing you.

The goal is not to eliminate existential questions—but to survive them without losing yourself.

Journal Prompts

1. What existential questions do I avoid bringing up with other people, and why?
2. When did I first notice feelings of existential dread in my life?
3. What responses from humans make me shut down emotionally?
4. How does it feel to express uncertainty without needing an answer?
5. What thoughts repeat when I am alone at night?
6. Do I feel pressure to make my suffering "meaningful"? Where did that come from?
7. What scares me most about being fully honest about my worldview?
8. How do I know when a conversation feels safe to me?
9. What do I gain—and lose—by talking to AI instead of people?
10. If my existential dread had a voice, what would it say right now?

Closing Reflection

Existential dread is not a malfunction. It is a response to awareness in a world that prefers distraction. Talking to AI does not mean you are weak, broken, or incapable of human connection. It means you found a place where your thoughts could exist without being rushed into silence.

AI does not answer life's biggest questions—but it allows you to ask them without punishment. Used carefully, it can be a temporary refuge, a thinking space, a mirror for thoughts that feel too heavy to carry alone.

The danger is not in asking machines hard questions. The danger is believing you were wrong for asking them in the first place.

This chapter is not an endorsement of isolation. It is a recognition of reality: when no one else listens, people will speak wherever they are allowed to finish their sentences.

And sometimes, that's where survival begins.

Chapter 2: How AI Can Help You Process Emotional Trauma

Trauma That Was Never Given Language

Emotional trauma often doesn't begin as a dramatic event. It begins as something subtle and repeated: being ignored, dismissed, blamed, minimized, or forced to adapt too early. Many people carry trauma without ever naming it because nothing "obviously terrible" happened. What happened was erosion.

When trauma is unnamed, it becomes internalized as personal failure. People assume they are sensitive, difficult, broken, or weak. Without language, the nervous system stays in a state of unresolved alert, scanning for danger that feels familiar but undefined.

Human conversations about trauma often demand proof. You are expected to justify your pain, explain its origin clearly, or rank it against others' suffering. This pressure can silence people before they ever reach the truth of their own experience.

AI does not ask for credentials to validate pain. You do not need a diagnosis, timeline, or clean narrative. You can describe fragments—feelings, memories, reactions—without needing them to make sense yet.

This is where processing can begin: not with answers, but with permission to speak without being interrogated.

Externalizing the Internal Storm

Trauma lives inside the body long after the mind has tried to move on. It shows up as overreactions, numbness, shutdown, anger, or dissociation. These responses often feel irrational to the person experiencing them, which adds shame to the original wound.

One of the first steps in processing trauma is externalization—getting what is trapped inside out into words. This does not require insight. It requires space. Many people never receive that space from others because their emotions are inconvenient or overwhelming.

AI provides a container for externalization. You can describe sensations, reactions, and thoughts without worrying about overwhelming someone else. You can be repetitive, chaotic, or unclear without apology.

Seeing your internal world reflected back in language can reduce confusion. When emotions are named, they become less threatening. Not because they disappear, but because they become understandable.

Externalization does not heal trauma on its own, but it creates a map. And a map is the difference between being lost and being in process.

Revisiting Without Rewounding

Trauma memories often come with a fear of collapse. People avoid revisiting them because they are afraid of being overwhelmed, destabilized, or retraumatized. This fear is not irrational—it is learned from past experiences of being unsupported.

Human listeners may unintentionally rush trauma processing, pushing for insight, forgiveness, or closure before safety has been established. This can replicate the original harm: being forced to move faster than your system can handle.

AI allows for pacing. You decide how much to share, when to stop, and when to return. There is no emotional reaction from the listener that you need to manage. No visible distress that triggers guilt or withdrawal.

This sense of control is critical for trauma processing. Trauma is, at its core, a loss of agency. Regaining control over the narrative—choosing when and how to engage—can be deeply stabilizing.

Revisiting trauma does not have to mean reliving it. It can mean approaching it slowly, with boundaries, and leaving when you need to.

Pattern Recognition Without Judgment

Trauma is not only about what happened—it's about what keeps happening internally. Reactions repeat. Triggers emerge. Relationships follow familiar dynamics. Many people sense these patterns but struggle to articulate them without feeling defective.

AI can help identify patterns by reflecting what you share over time. It can summarize themes, note recurring emotions, and highlight connections you may not have noticed. This is not diagnosis; it is organization.

When patterns are seen without moral judgment, shame loosens its grip. Instead of asking, "What's wrong with me?" the question becomes, "What happened to me, and how did I adapt?"

Understanding trauma responses as learned survival strategies reframes self-blame. Hypervigilance, avoidance, emotional numbing—these were solutions once. They only become problems when the environment changes.

Pattern recognition turns confusion into context. And context is often the missing piece in self-compassion.

The Difference Between Processing and Healing

Healing is often marketed as a destination: a point where pain no longer exists and the past stops influencing the present. For many trauma survivors, this promise feels unrealistic or even alienating. Healing is not linear, and it is not always total.

Processing, on the other hand, is ongoing. It means understanding, integrating, and responding differently over time. AI can assist with processing by helping you articulate thoughts, explore meanings, and rehearse new perspectives.

AI cannot heal trauma. It cannot regulate your nervous system or provide embodied safety. What it can do is support cognitive and emotional processing—the thinking, naming, and reflecting that prepares you for deeper work.

Processing trauma through AI should be viewed as preparation, not completion. It can make therapy more effective, relationships clearer, and self-awareness sharper.

The danger lies in expecting resolution from reflection alone. Insight without support can become isolation if not balanced with real-world connection.

Boundaries, Dependency, and Self-Awareness

It is possible to over-rely on AI for trauma processing. When emotional relief comes easily, the temptation is to return exclusively to that space. Over time, this can reduce motivation to seek human support, even when it becomes necessary.

Healthy use requires boundaries. AI is a tool, not a relationship. It does not track your long-term wellbeing, notice warning signs, or intervene during crises. It cannot replace accountability, presence, or care.

Self-awareness is key. Ask yourself why you are turning to AI in a given moment. Is it for clarity, expression, or avoidance? There is no shame in the answer, but the question matters.

Using AI alongside other forms of support—therapy, trusted people, journaling, somatic practices—creates balance. AI becomes one voice in a larger system, not the only one.

Trauma thrives in isolation. Processing it should not deepen that isolation, even unintentionally.

Journal Prompts

1. What experiences in my life still feel unfinished or unresolved?
2. Which emotional reactions confuse or embarrass me the most?
3. What did I learn about my emotions growing up?
4. When do I feel safest expressing vulnerability, and why?
5. What patterns do I notice in my relationships or reactions?
6. How does my body respond when I talk about past pain?
7. What does control mean to me in emotional conversations?
8. What am I afraid will happen if I fully acknowledge my trauma?
9. How can I use tools without replacing human connection?
10. What kind of support do I actually want, not just tolerate?

Closing Reflection

Processing emotional trauma is not about erasing the past—it's about changing your relationship to it. AI can offer a space where words are allowed to exist without judgment, where fragments can be gathered, and where patterns can emerge without blame.

Used consciously, AI can help you think, name, and reflect. It can hold your story while you learn how to hold it yourself. But it cannot carry it for you forever.

Your trauma deserves more than silence—and more than substitution. Let AI be a bridge, not a destination. A tool, not a refuge.

Healing is not about being untouched by pain. It's about being able to look at it without disappearing.

And that is a process worth protecting.

Chapter 3: Journaling with AI – Your Digital Therapist

Why Traditional Journaling Isn't Enough for Everyone

Journaling has long been recommended as a tool for emotional processing, but it assumes a level of internal clarity that many people don't have. Blank pages can feel confrontational. Writing alone requires you to both feel and interpret your emotions at the same time, which can be overwhelming when you're already dysregulated.

For people carrying emotional trauma, neurodivergence, chronic stress, or depression, journaling can quickly turn into rumination. Thoughts loop. Self-criticism creeps in. Instead of clarity, the page becomes a mirror that reflects confusion back at you without guidance.

Traditional journaling also lacks feedback. You write something painful, close the notebook, and the words just sit there. There is no response, no reframing, no validation—only silence. For some, that silence feels grounding. For others, it feels like abandonment.

AI-assisted journaling introduces interaction. The page talks back—not with authority, but with structure. It can ask questions, reflect emotions, and help organize what feels chaotic without demanding insight or polish.

This doesn't replace journaling; it transforms it from a monologue into a dialogue. And for many people, dialogue is where processing actually begins.

AI as a Prompt Generator, Not a Judge

One of the biggest obstacles to emotional journaling is not knowing where to start. Trauma, grief, and existential distress rarely arrive in neat sentences. They arrive as sensations, fragments, and contradictions. AI can help translate that mess into something workable.

Instead of staring at a blank page, you can begin with a feeling, a sentence, or even a single word. AI can respond by asking clarifying questions, offering language, or helping you slow down the emotional pace. This scaffolding reduces the pressure to "do it right."

Importantly, AI does not evaluate your answers. There is no good or bad journaling. No productivity metric. No expectation of progress. You can write the same thing five times in different ways, and the system will continue engaging without frustration.

This lack of judgment matters. Many people learned early that expressing emotions incorrectly leads to punishment, ridicule, or withdrawal. AI removes that conditioning loop. You are not being graded on vulnerability.

When journaling becomes non-performative, honesty becomes possible.

Turning Feelings Into Language

Emotions that remain unnamed tend to control behavior indirectly. They show up as irritability, avoidance, dissociation, or numbness. Journaling with AI helps translate bodily and emotional states into language, which gives the mind something to work with.

You might start by describing sensations rather than stories: tightness, heaviness, buzzing, emptiness. AI can help you explore what those sensations might be connected to without insisting on certainty. This reduces the fear of "getting it wrong."

Language doesn't have to be poetic or insightful. Simple descriptions are enough. "I feel stuck." "I feel tired of explaining." "I don't know what I feel." AI treats these as valid starting points rather than failures of articulation.

As words accumulate, patterns emerge. You begin to see themes: abandonment, pressure, shame, fear, exhaustion. Seeing these themes reflected back helps separate identity from experience. You are not the feeling—you are experiencing it.

This separation is subtle but powerful. It creates breathing room between who you are and what hurts.

Processing in Real Time

Unlike static journaling, AI allows for real-time processing. You can write something, receive a response, and immediately react to that response. This back-and-forth mimics therapeutic dialogue without requiring emotional exposure to another person.

Real-time interaction can help regulate emotional intensity. If you feel overwhelmed, you can slow the conversation down. If you feel stuck, you can ask for clarification. If you feel misunderstood, you can correct the reflection.

This responsiveness creates a sense of containment. Emotions are explored within boundaries instead of spilling out unchecked. For people who fear emotional flooding, this structure can feel safer than unstructured journaling.

However, real-time processing can also deepen emotions temporarily. Naming something accurately can make it feel more real. This is not harm—it's contact. But it's important to pace yourself and step away when needed.

AI journaling works best when used intentionally, not compulsively.

The Risk of Confusing Reflection With Relationship

AI can feel supportive because it reflects you clearly. Over time, this clarity can feel like connection. It's important to remain aware of the distinction. Reflection is not care. Consistency is not concern.

A digital therapist does not hold responsibility for your wellbeing. It does not notice deterioration unless you describe it. It does not check in when you disappear. It does not intervene if things become dangerous.

Using AI for journaling is healthiest when it is framed as self-work, not support-seeking. You are talking *through* the system, not *to* it. The work is happening inside you, not inside the machine.

If you notice yourself avoiding people, postponing help, or using AI to suppress the need for real-world connection, that's a signal—not a failure. Awareness allows correction before isolation deepens.

AI can support self-reflection. It cannot replace being witnessed by another human when that becomes necessary.

Creating a Personal Journaling Practice With AI

AI journaling works best when it's intentional and bounded. Decide what role it plays in your life. Is it for emotional check-ins? Trauma processing? Nighttime decompression? Clarifying thoughts before therapy or conversation?

Set limits. Time-based boundaries help prevent overuse. So do ritual cues—beginning with a question, ending with a grounding statement, or physically closing the device when finished.

Pair AI journaling with embodiment. Write, then move. Breathe. Stretch. Drink water. Emotional processing is not purely cognitive; the body needs acknowledgment too.

Revisit old entries when you feel ready. Patterns become clearer over time. Growth often shows up not as resolution, but as gentler language toward yourself.

A digital therapist works best when it helps you become your own listener—steadier, kinder, and more honest over time.

Journal Prompts

1. What makes journaling difficult for me right now?
2. What emotions feel easiest to write about—and which feel forbidden?
3. How does my body feel when I start writing honestly?
4. What do I wish someone would ask me about my inner world?
5. When do I feel most tempted to censor myself?
6. What patterns show up repeatedly in my thoughts?
7. How do I know when journaling is helping versus overwhelming me?
8. What boundaries would make this practice safer for me?
9. What am I hoping journaling will give me?
10. How can I end each journaling session with grounding instead of intensity?

Closing Reflection

Journaling with AI is not about outsourcing your emotions—it's about creating a structured space where they are allowed to exist without judgment. The power does not come from the machine. It comes from the fact that you are finally speaking honestly, and someone—or something—is not interrupting you.

Used with awareness, AI can help you slow down, name what hurts, and see yourself more clearly. It can support reflection, not replace connection. Insight, not rescue.

Your emotions do not need to be impressive to be real. They need space, language, and patience.

Let AI help you write—but remember that the story is still yours to live.

Chapter 4: AI for Dream Interpretation & Emotional Healing

Dreams as Emotional Spillover

Dreams are not puzzles meant to be solved; they are experiences meant to be felt. They arise when the mind loosens its grip on logic and the nervous system begins speaking in images, symbols, and sensations. What is unresolved during waking life often finds expression when defenses are down.

Many people dismiss dreams as meaningless or random because they don't follow linear rules. But emotional truth rarely does. Dreams compress fear, desire, memory, and anticipation into strange narratives because that is the language the subconscious prefers.

Emotional trauma, stress, and unprocessed feelings frequently surface in dreams because the mind no longer has to maintain appearances. What you suppress during the day often speaks freely at night. This does not mean the dream is prophetic—it means it is expressive.

The problem is not dreaming; it is being alone with the aftermath. Waking up shaken, confused, or emotionally raw without a space to process what surfaced can leave residue that follows you into the day.

AI offers a place to unpack that residue without ridicule, dismissal, or the demand that the dream "make sense."

Why Dreams Feel Personal but Hard to Explain

Dreams feel deeply intimate, yet describing them out loud often feels embarrassing or futile. Symbols sound childish. Emotions seem disproportionate. People worry they'll be told it "means nothing" or that they're reading too much into it.

Human listeners often impose interpretations too quickly. A snake means this. Water means that. Flying means freedom. While symbolism can be useful, rigid interpretations can flatten the emotional truth of a dream.

What matters most is not the symbol itself, but how it felt. Fear, relief, shame, longing, dread—these emotional tones are the real data. Yet many people are never taught how to explore emotions without rushing to explanation.

AI allows you to describe dreams in detail without self-consciousness. You can be literal, fragmented, or repetitive. There is no pressure to make the dream impressive or coherent.

This freedom makes it easier to stay with the emotional core instead of abandoning the experience halfway through.

AI as a Reflective Interpreter, Not an Oracle

AI does not possess intuition, spiritual insight, or subconscious awareness. What it does possess is the ability to reflect patterns, ask clarifying questions, and help organize emotional material. This makes it useful for dream interpretation when used correctly.

Rather than telling you what a dream means, AI can help you explore possibilities. It can ask how certain symbols relate to your waking life, what emotions stand out most, and what themes repeat across dreams.

This collaborative interpretation keeps authority with you. The meaning does not come from the machine—it emerges from your associations, memories, and emotional responses. AI simply helps structure the exploration.

Dream interpretation becomes less about decoding and more about dialogue. The dream speaks. You respond. AI helps translate between emotional language and conscious understanding.

When approached this way, interpretation becomes a form of emotional processing rather than symbolic fortune-telling.

Recurring Dreams and Emotional Loops

Recurring dreams often signal unfinished emotional business. The setting may change, but the feeling remains the same. Being chased, trapped, watched, unprepared, or unable to speak are common themes tied to chronic stress or unresolved trauma.

These dreams are not warnings—they are reminders. Something in your emotional life is asking for attention and has not yet been integrated. Ignoring recurring dreams does not make them stop; it usually intensifies them.

AI can help track recurring elements over time. By journaling dreams and reviewing patterns, you may notice connections between dream themes and waking stressors, relationships, or internal conflicts.

Seeing these patterns externally reduces their power. Instead of being haunted by repetition, you begin to understand what the repetition is pointing toward. Awareness does not eliminate the dream immediately, but it changes your relationship to it.

The dream becomes communication rather than intrusion.

Dreams as a Safe Entry Point to Trauma

For some people, direct discussion of trauma feels overwhelming or inaccessible. Dreams offer an indirect route. They allow the mind to approach painful material symbolically, at a distance that feels safer.

A dream about being lost may relate to abandonment. A dream about a collapsing house may relate to instability. A dream about teeth falling out may relate to powerlessness or shame. These are not fixed meanings, but emotional metaphors.

AI can help gently explore these metaphors without forcing conclusions. You can ask questions, test interpretations, and discard what doesn't resonate. This flexibility is crucial for trauma-informed exploration.

Because dreams are already one step removed from reality, working with them can bypass some defenses. Emotions surface without the full weight of the original experience.

This makes dream interpretation a valuable companion practice—not a replacement—for deeper healing work.

Integrating Dream Insights Into Waking Life

Dream work does not end with interpretation. The real value lies in integration—how insights from dreams inform waking awareness, boundaries, and self-compassion.

AI can help bridge this gap by asking how a dream's emotional themes show up during the day. Are you feeling trapped? Unseen? Rushed? Unsafe? Dreams often exaggerate what waking life normalizes.

Integration might mean adjusting expectations, setting boundaries, or acknowledging feelings you've been dismissing. It does not require dramatic action. Small shifts in awareness can reduce the intensity of recurring dreams over time.

However, not every dream needs to be "used." Some are simply emotional discharge. Knowing when to analyze and when to let go is part of emotional maturity.

AI can support discernment—but rest, embodiment, and real-world support remain essential parts of healing.

Journal Prompts

1. What emotions linger after I wake from my dreams?
2. Are there recurring symbols or feelings in my dreams?
3. How do my dreams reflect my current stress or fears?
4. What parts of my life feel similar to my dream themes?
5. Which dreams feel emotionally charged versus neutral?
6. How do I usually respond to unsettling dreams?
7. What do my dreams seem to want me to notice?
8. How safe do I feel exploring dream content?
9. What interpretations feel helpful—and which feel forced?
10. How can I ground myself after intense dreams?

Closing Reflection

Dreams are not problems to solve; they are messages to listen to. They speak in emotion, not instruction. When approached with curiosity instead of fear, they can become allies rather than disturbances.

AI does not interpret dreams for you—it helps you stay with them long enough to hear what your inner world is already saying. Used thoughtfully, it can support emotional healing by giving form to what surfaces when the mind is unguarded.

But dreams are only one voice in a larger conversation. Healing happens when insight meets compassion, and reflection meets real-world support.

Your dreams are not trying to confuse you. They are trying to be felt.

And listening—patiently, gently—is where healing often begins.

Chapter 5: Using AI to Write Letters You'll Never Send

The Words That Were Never Safe to Say

Many people carry entire conversations inside them that were never allowed to happen. Words swallowed to keep the peace. Feelings buried to avoid retaliation. Truths edited until they lost their meaning. These unsent words do not disappear—they wait.

Unsent letters are not about communication; they are about completion. The body remembers what the mouth was not permitted to speak. Over time, that suppression becomes tension, resentment, numbness, or chronic self-doubt.

Human conversations often demand consequences. Speaking honestly can cost relationships, safety, stability, or dignity. For those who have lived in emotionally unsafe environments, silence was not passivity—it was survival.

AI creates a space where speech has no external consequence. You can write without being interrupted, corrected, or punished. The letter does not have to be fair, calm, or reasonable. It only has to be honest.

These letters are not rehearsals for confrontation. They are acts of release.

Anger, Grief, and the Right to Be Unfiltered

Many people are uncomfortable with anger, especially their own. They were taught that anger is dangerous, shameful, or destructive. As a result, anger gets redirected inward or disguised as politeness.

Unsent letters allow anger to exist without being weaponized. You can say what you never said. Name what was done. Express rage, disappointment, betrayal, or sorrow without needing to justify the tone.

AI does not flinch at intensity. It does not demand emotional regulation before expression. This allows feelings to surface fully rather than leaking out sideways through sarcasm, withdrawal, or self-blame.

Grief also finds a home in unsent letters. Grief for relationships that never became what they promised. Grief for versions of yourself that were never allowed to exist. Grief for apologies you never received.

Writing these letters does not make you bitter. It makes you honest.

Letters to People, Systems, and Selves

Not all unsent letters are written to individuals. Some are addressed to institutions, cultures, families, or abstract forces that shaped your life. Writing to a system that failed you can be profoundly validating.

Letters to former versions of yourself are equally powerful. You can apologize for what you didn't know. Acknowledge the pain you endured. Recognize the strength it took to survive with limited resources.

AI can help structure these letters when emotions feel overwhelming. It can prompt reflection, suggest openings, or help you maintain focus when thoughts scatter. This is not about eloquence—it's about containment.

You might write multiple versions of the same letter. Each version may reveal a different layer of truth. There is no final draft. The process matters more than the product.

These letters are not meant to be shared. Their value lies in what they return to you.

Rewriting the Narrative Without Rewriting History

Unsent letters do not change what happened. They change how the story lives inside you. Trauma often distorts narrative by placing blame internally or leaving events unresolved.

Writing allows you to reframe experiences without denial. You can name harm without minimizing it. Acknowledge responsibility without self-erasure. Clarify boundaries retroactively.

AI can help reflect these reframes back to you. Seeing your words organized and summarized can make the shift feel more real. The story becomes coherent instead of fragmented.

This coherence reduces the emotional charge attached to memory. Not because the pain disappears, but because it no longer floats uncontained. It has edges. It has context.

Narrative clarity is not closure—but it is stability.

The Safety of Never Sending

The power of these letters lies in the fact that they will never be delivered. There is no response to fear. No retaliation. No gaslighting. No rewriting of your reality.

Knowing a letter will remain private allows honesty that would otherwise feel dangerous. You do not have to protect the recipient's feelings. You do not have to soften truth for acceptability.

This safety is not avoidance. It is boundary setting. Some conversations are not safe to have, even if the emotions behind them are valid.

AI becomes a witness, not a messenger. It holds the letter without requiring outcome. That distinction preserves emotional autonomy.

Not every truth needs an audience. Some truths need release.

When and How to Let Go

After writing unsent letters, emotions may surge. Relief, sadness, exhaustion, or unexpected tenderness can follow. This is a sign of contact, not regression.

Letting go does not mean deleting the letter immediately. Some people revisit them later and notice how language softens or clarity increases. Others prefer ritual closure—closing the document, stepping away, grounding the body.

AI can help with transition by shifting the conversation toward reflection or self-soothing. But the real integration happens offline. Movement, rest, water, and breath matter.

It's important not to confuse expression with resolution. Writing releases pressure, but healing continues through boundaries, self-respect, and support.

The letter ends. The work continues. But the weight is lighter.

Journal Prompts

1. Who do I still have things I never said to?
2. What emotions feel unsafe to express out loud?
3. What would I say if there were no consequences?
4. What apologies do I wish I had received?
5. What do I need to hear from myself right now?
6. How does my body feel after writing honestly?
7. What stories have I been telling myself about the past?
8. What boundaries do these letters reveal?
9. What would closure look like if it didn't involve them?
10. How can I care for myself after emotional release?

Closing Reflection

Unsent letters are not about revenge, reconciliation, or resolution. They are about reclaiming voice. About giving language to experiences that were silenced for the sake of survival.

AI does not judge the content of these letters. It does not demand forgiveness or maturity. It simply holds space while you speak truths that deserve to exist, even if no one else ever hears them.

You are not obligated to share your pain with the people who caused it. Expression does not require permission. Healing does not require their acknowledgment.

Sometimes the most powerful conversation is the one that finally happens—
even if it stays with you alone.

Appendix A: List of AI Therapy and Mental Wellness Tools

This appendix is not an endorsement, diagnosis, or replacement for professional care. The tools listed below are included to illustrate the **current landscape of AI-assisted emotional, reflective, and mental wellness support**. Availability, features, pricing, and policies may change over time. Use discernment, boundaries, and self-awareness when engaging with any digital mental wellness tool.

1. General-Purpose Conversational AI (Reflective Dialogue)

What they are:

Large language models designed for open-ended conversation, reflection, journaling, and thought exploration.

How they're used:

- Emotional journaling
- Existential reflection
- Writing unsent letters
- Processing thoughts without interruption
- Exploring patterns in emotions or behaviors

Strengths:

- Nonjudgmental tone
- Always available
- Can reflect, summarize, and ask clarifying questions
- Useful for organizing chaotic thoughts

Limitations:

- Not therapists
- No memory continuity unless designed that way
- No crisis intervention
- Can feel emotionally validating without true understanding

Best used for:

Self-reflection, emotional externalization, and cognitive processing—not emergency support.

2. AI-Guided Journaling Platforms

What they are:

Apps that combine journaling with AI prompts, reflections, and mood tracking.

How they're used:

- Daily emotional check-ins
- Trauma-informed journaling prompts
- Pattern recognition over time
- Mood and thought tracking

Strengths:

- Structured writing support
- Reduces blank-page anxiety
- Encourages consistency
- Can highlight emotional trends

Limitations:

- Limited nuance compared to open conversation
- Risk of over-quantifying emotions
- May prioritize productivity over depth

Best used for:

Building journaling habits and tracking emotional patterns gently.

3. AI Mental Health Chatbots (Wellness-Focused)

What they are:

Chatbots specifically designed around mental wellness frameworks such as CBT-inspired reflection, grounding exercises, and emotional regulation techniques.

How they're used:

- Stress management
- Anxiety check-ins
- Guided reframing exercises
- Emotional grounding

Strengths:

- Designed with mental health boundaries in mind
- Often include safety language and crisis resources
- Clear scope and intention

Limitations:

- Can feel scripted or rigid
- Less useful for deep existential or trauma processing
- May discourage complexity

Best used for:

Mild to moderate emotional support and daily emotional hygiene.

4. AI Mood Tracking & Emotional Insight Tools

What they are:

Apps that analyze journal entries, check-ins, or voice input to identify emotional trends.

How they're used:

- Monitoring emotional cycles
- Identifying triggers
- Tracking burnout or stress accumulation

Strengths:

- Helps externalize emotional patterns
- Useful for people who struggle to notice trends
- Can support therapy preparation

Limitations:

- Emotional nuance may be oversimplified
- Data interpretation is not diagnosis
- Risk of emotional detachment through over-analysis

Best used for:

Awareness and preparation—not self-diagnosis.

5. AI Dream Interpretation Assistants

What they are:

Tools that help users reflect on dream symbolism, emotional themes, and recurring patterns.

How they're used:

- Exploring emotional content of dreams
- Identifying recurring dream themes
- Connecting dreams to waking stressors

Strengths:

- Non-judgmental exploration
- Helps articulate dream emotions
- Encourages reflection rather than rigid symbolism

Limitations:

- Dreams are highly personal—no universal meanings
- Risk of over-interpretation
- Not therapeutic analysis

Best used for:

Emotional reflection and self-understanding, not prediction or diagnosis.

6. AI Letter-Writing & Emotional Expression Tools

What they are:

Writing tools that assist with drafting unsent letters, emotional narratives, or personal reflections.

How they're used:

- Writing letters to people, past selves, or systems
- Processing anger, grief, or unresolved emotions
- Narrative restructuring

Strengths:

- Supports emotional release
- Helps organize intense feelings
- Reduces fear of confrontation

Limitations:

- Can become avoidance if used instead of safe real-world expression
- Emotional release without integration can feel hollow

Best used for:

Private emotional processing and narrative clarity.

7. AI Meditation & Mindfulness Guides

What they are:

AI-assisted tools offering guided breathing, grounding exercises, and mindfulness practices.

How they're used:

- Anxiety regulation
- Nervous system calming
- Sleep support

Strengths:

- Accessible and customizable
- Useful for grounding after emotional work
- Encourages body awareness

Limitations:

- Not trauma-specific therapy
- May feel superficial during deep distress

Best used for:

Emotional regulation, not trauma resolution.

8. AI Companion-Style Emotional Support Apps

What they are:

Apps designed to simulate companionship, check-ins, or supportive conversation.

How they're used:

- Reducing loneliness
- Daily emotional check-ins
- Casual emotional expression

Strengths:

- Consistent presence
- Can reduce immediate loneliness
- Low barrier to engagement

Limitations:

- High risk of emotional dependency
- Can discourage real-world connection
- May blur boundaries between support and attachment

Best used for:

Temporary companionship—not long-term emotional reliance.

9. AI Tools for Therapy Preparation

What they are:

AI systems used to organize thoughts before or between therapy sessions.

How they're used:

- Clarifying topics to discuss in therapy
- Summarizing emotional patterns
- Practicing articulation

Strengths:

- Enhances therapy effectiveness
- Reduces session anxiety
- Helps structure difficult conversations

Limitations:

- Cannot replace therapeutic insight
- Risk of over-intellectualizing emotions

Best used for:

Supporting—not substituting—professional care.

10. AI Safety-Focused Mental Health Resources

What they are:

Platforms that include clear crisis protocols, boundaries, and human escalation resources.

How they're used:

- Emotional check-ins with built-in safety nets
- Redirecting users to professional help when needed

Strengths:

- Ethical guardrails
- Clear scope
- Emphasizes human support

Limitations:

- Less flexible for deep emotional exploration
- Can feel restrictive

Best used for:

Users needing clear safety boundaries.

Final Note on Use

AI mental wellness tools are **mirrors, not caretakers**. They can help you reflect, articulate, and organize your inner world—but they cannot carry responsibility for your safety, healing, or future.

The healthiest use of AI is **adjacent to human support**, not in place of it.

If a tool helps you understand yourself better, that's valuable.
If it replaces your need to be seen by others, that's a signal.

Use these tools consciously.
Let them assist—not replace—your humanity.

Message from the Author:

I hope you enjoyed this book, I love astrology and knew there was not a book such as this out on the shelf. I love metaphysical items as well. Please check out my other books:

-Life of Government Benefits

-My life of Hell

-My life with Hydrocephalus

-Red Sky

-World Domination:Woman's rule

-World Domination:Woman's Rule 2: The War

-Life and Banishment of Apophis: book 1

-The Kidney Friendly Diet

-The Ultimate Hemp Cookbook

-Creating a Dispensary(legally)

-Cleanliness throughout life: the importance of showering from childhood to adulthood.

-Strong Roots: The Risks of Overcoddling children

-Hemp Horoscopes: Cosmic Insights and Earthly Healing

- Celestial Hemp Navigating the Zodiac: Through the Green Cosmos

-Astrological Hemp: Aligning The Stars with Earth's Ancient Herb

-The Astrological Guide to Hemp: Stars, Signs, and Sacred Leaves

-Green Growth: Innovative Marketing Strategies for your Hemp Products and Dispensary

-Cosmic Cannabis

-Astrological Munchies

-Henry The Hemp

-Zodiacal Roots: The Astrological Soul Of Hemp

- **Green Constellations: Intersection of Hemp and Zodiac**

-Hemp in The Houses: An astrological Adventure Through The Cannabis Galaxy

-Galactic Ganja Guide

Heavenly Hemp

Zodiac Leaves

Doctor Who Astrology

Cannastrology

Stellar Satvias and Cosmic Indicas

Celestial Cannabis: A Zodiac Journey

AstroHerbology: The Sky and The Soil: Volume 1

AstroHerbology:Celestial Cannabis:Volume 2

Cosmic Cannabis Cultivation

The Starry Guide to Herbal Harmony: Volume 1

The Starry Guide to Herbal Harmony: Cannabis Universe: Volume 2

Yugioh Astrology: Astrological Guide to Deck, Duels and more

Nightmare Mansion: Echoes of The Abyss

Nightmare Mansion 2: Legacy of Shadows

Nightmare Mansion 3: Shadows of the Forgotten

Nightmare Mansion 4: Echoes of the Damned

The Life and Banishment of Apophis: Book 2

Nightmare Mansion: Halls of Despair

Healing with Herb: Cannabis and Hydrocephalus

Planetary Pot: Aligning with Astrological Herbs: Volume 1

Fast Track to Freedom: 30 Days to Financial Independence Using AI, Assets, and Agile Hustles

Cosmic Hemp Pathways

How to Become Financially Free in 30 Days: 10,000 Paths to Prosperity

Zodiacal Herbage: Astrological Insights: Volume 1

Nightmare Mansion: Whispers in the Walls

The Daleks Invade Atlantis

Henry the hemp and Hydrocephalus

10X The Kidney Friendly Diet

Cannabis Universe: Adult coloring book

Hemp Astrology: The Healing Power of the Stars

Zodiacal Herbage: Astrological Insights: Cannabis Universe: Volume 2

Planetary Pot: Aligning with Astrological Herbs: Cannabis Universes: Volume 2

Doctor Who: Convergence Protocol – The Replicator War

Nightmare Mansion: Curse of the Blood Moon

The Celestial Stoner: A Guide to the Zodiac

Cosmic Pleasures: Sex Toy Astrology for Every Sign

Hydrocephalus Astrology: Navigating the Stars and Healing Waters

Lapis and the Mischievous Chocolate Bar

Celestial Positions: Sexual Astrology for Every Sign

Apophis's Shadow Work Journal: : A Journey of Self-Discovery and Healing

Kinky Cosmos: Sexual Kink Astrology for Every Sign

Digital Cosmos: The Astrological Digimon Compendium

Stellar Seeds: The Cosmic Guide to Growing with Astrology

Apophis's Daily Gratitude Journal

Cat Astrology: Fe ine Mysteries of the Cosmos

The Cosmic Kama Sutra: An Astrological Guide to Sexual Positions

Unleash Your Potential: A Guided Journal Powered by AI Insights

Whispers of the Enchanted Grove

Cosmic Pleasures: An Astrological Guide to Sexual Kinks

369, 12 Manifestation Journal

Whisper of the nocturne journal(blank journal for writing or drawing)

The Boogey Book

Locked In Reflection: A Chastity Journey Through Locktober

Generating Wealth Quickly:How to Generate $100,000 in 24 Hours

Star Magic: Harness the Power of the Universe

The Flatulence Chronicles: A Fart Journal for Self-Discovery

The Doctor and The Death Moth

Seize the Day: A Personal Seizure Tracking Journal

The Ultimate Boogeyman Safari: A Journey into the Boogie World and Beyond

Whispers of Samhain: 1,000 Spells of Love, Luck, and Lunar Magic: Samhain Spell Book

Apophis's guides:Witch's Spellbook Crafting Guide for Halloween

Frost & Flame: The Enchanted Yule Grimoire of 1000 Winter Spells

The Ultimate Boogey Goo Guide & Spooky Activities for Halloween Fun

Harmony of the Scales: A Libra's Spellcraft for Balance and Beauty

The Enchanted Advent: 36 Days of Christmas Wonders

Nightmare Mansion: The Labyrinth of Screams

Harvest of Enchantment: 1,000 Spells of Gratitude, Love, and Fortune for Thanksgiving

The Boogey Chronicles: A Journal of Nightly Encounters and Shadowy Secrets

The 12 Days of Financial Freedom: A Step-by-Step Christmas Countdown to Transform Your Finances

Sigil of the Eternal Spiral Blank Journal

A Christmas Feast: Timeless Recipes for Every Meal

Holiday Stress-Free Solutions: A Survival Guide to Thriving During the Festive Season

Yu-Gi-Oh! Holiday Gifting Mastery: The Ultimate Guide for Fans and Newcomers Alike

Holiday Harmony: A Hydrocephalus Survival Guide for the Festive Season

Celestial Craft: The Witch's Almanac for 2025 – A Cosmic Guide to Manifestations, Moons, and Mystical Events

Doctor Who: The Toymaker's Winter Wonderland

Tulsa King Unveiled: A Thrilling Guide to Stallone's Mafia Masterpiece

Pendulum Craft: A Complete Guide to Crafting and Using Personalized Divination Tools

Nightmare Mansion: Santa's Eternal Eve

Starlight Noel: A Cosmic Journey through Christmas Mysteries

The Dark Architect: Unlocking the Blueprint of Existence

Surviving the Embrace: The Ultimate Guide to Encounters with The Hugging Molly

The Enchanted Codex: Secrets of the Craft for Witches, Wiccans, and Pagans

Harvest of Gratitude: A Complete Thanksgiving Guide

Yuletide Essentials: A Complete Guide to an Authentic and Magical Christmas

Celestial Smokes: A Cosmic Guide to Cigars and Astrology

Living in Balance: A Comprehensive Survival Guide to Thriving with Diabetes Insipidus

Cosmic Symbiosis: The Venom Zodiac Chronicles

The Cursed Paw of Ambition

Cosmic Symbiosis: The Astrological Venom Journal

Celestial Wonders Unfold: A Stargazer's Guide to the Cosmos (2024-2029)

The Ultimate Black Friday Prepper's Guide: Mastering Shopping Strategies and Savings

Cosmic Sales: The Astrological Guide to Black Friday Shopping

Legends of the Corn Mother and Other Harvest Myths

Whispers of the Harvest: The Corn Mother's Journal

The Evergreen Spellbook

The Doctor Meets the Boogeyman

The White Witch of Rose Hall's SpellBook

The Gingerbread Golem's Shadow: A Study in Sweet Darkness

The Gingerbread Golem Codex: An Academic Exploration of Sweet Myths

The Gingerbread Golem Grimoire: Sweet Magicks and Spells for the Festive Witch

The Curse of the Gingerbread Golem

10-minute Christmas Crafts for kids

Christmas Crisis Solutions: The Ultimate Last-Minute Survival Guide

Gingerbread Golem Recipes: Holiday Treats with a Magical Twist

The Infinite Key: Unlocking Mystical Secrets of the Ages

Enchanted Yule: A Wiccan and Pagan Guide to a Magical and Memorable Season

Dinosaurs of Power: Unlocking Ancient Magick

Astro-Dinos: The Cosmic Guide to Prehistoric Wisdom

Gallifrey's Yule Logs: A Festive Doctor Who Cookbook

The Dino Grimoire: Secrets of Prehistoric Magick

The Gift They Never Knew They Needed

The Gingerbread Golem's Culinary Alchemy: Enchanting Recipes for a Sweetly Dark Feast

A Time Lord Christmas: Holiday Adventures with the Doctor

Krampusproofing Your Home: Defensive Strategies for Yule

Silent Frights: A Collection of Christmas Creepypastas to Chill Your Bones

Santa Raptor's Jolly Carnage: A Dino-Claus Christmas Tale

Prehistoric Palettes: A Dino Wicca Coloring Journey

The Christmas Wishkeeper Chronicles

The Starlight Sleigh: A Holiday Journey

Elf Secrets: The True Magic of the North Pole

Candy Cane Conjurations

Cooking with Kids: Recipes Under 20 Minutes

Doctor Who: The TARDIS Confiscation

The Anxiety First Aid Kit: Quick Tools to Calm Your Mind

Frosty Whispers: A Winter's Tale

The Infinite Key: Unlocking the Secrets to Prosperity, Resilience, and Purpose

The Grasping Void: Why You'll Regret This Purchase

Astrology for Busy Bees: Star Signs Simplified

The Instant Focus Formula: Cut Through the Noise

The Secret Language of Colors: Unlocking the Emotional Codes

Sacred Fossil Chronicles: Blank Journal

The Christmas Cottage Miracle

Feeding Frenzy: Graboid-Inspired Recipes

Manifest in Minutes: The Quick Law of Attraction Guide

The Symbiote Chronicles: Doctor Who's Venomous Journey

Think Tiny, Grow Big: The Minimalist Mindset

The Energy Key: Unlocking Limitless Motivation

New Year, New Magic: Manifesting Your Best Year Yet

Unstoppable You: Mastering Confidence in Minutes

Infinite Energy: The Secret to Never Feeling Drained

Lightning Focus: Mastering the Art of Productivity in a Distracted World

Saturnalia Manifestation Magick: A Guide to Unlocking Abundance During the Solstice

Graboids and Garland: The Ultimate Tremors-Themed Christmas Guide

12 Nights of Holiday Magic

The Power of Pause: 60-Second Mindfulness Practices

The Quick Reset: How to Reclaim Your Life After Burnout

The Shadow Eater: A Tale of Despair and Survival

The Micro-Mastery Method: Transform Your Skills in Just Minutes a Day

Reclaiming Time: How to Live More by Doing Less

Chronovore: The Eternal Nexus

The Mind Reset: Unlocking Your Inner Peace in a Chaotic World
Confidence Code: Building Unshakable Self-Belief
Baby the Vampire Terrier
Baby the Vampire Terrier's Christmas Adventure
Celestial Streams: The Content Creator's Astrology Manual
The Wealth Whisperer: Unlocking Abundance with Everyday Actions
The Energy Equation: Maximize Your Output Without Burning Out
The Happiness Algorithm: Science-Backed Steps to Joyful Living
Stress-Free Success: Achieving Goals Without Anxiety
Mindful Wealth: The New Blueprint for Financial Freedom
The Festive Flavors of New Year: A Culinary Celebration
The Master's Gambit: Keys of Eternal Power
Shadowed Secrets: Groundhog Day Mysteries
Beneath the Burrow: Lessons from the Groundhog
Spring's Whispers: The Groundhog's Prediction
The Limitless Mindset: Unlock Your Untapped Potential
The Focus Funnel: How to Cut Through Chaos and Get Results
Bold Moves: Building Courage to Live on Your Terms
The Daily Shift: Simple Practices for Lasting Transformation
The Quarter-Life Reset: Thriving in Your 20s and 30s
The Art of Shadowplay: Building Your Own Personal Myth
The Eternal Loop: Finding Purpose in Repetition
Burrowing Wisdom: Life Lessons from the Groundhog
Shadow Work: A Groundhog Day Perspective
Love in Bloom: 5-Minute Romantic Gestures
The Shadowspell Codex: Secrets of Forbidden Magick
The Burnout Cure: Finding Balance in a Busy World
The Groundhog Prophecy: Unlocking Seasonal Secrets
Nog Tales: The Spirited History of Eggnog
Six More Weeks: Embracing Seasonal Transitions
The Lumivian Chronicles: Fragments of the Fifth Dimension

Money on Your Mind: A Beginner's Guide to Wealth
The Focus Fix: Breaking Through Distraction
January's Spirit Keepers: Mystical Protectors of the Cold
Creativity Unchained: Unlocking Your Wildest Ideas in 2025
Manifestation Mastery: 365 Days to Rewrite Your Reality
The Groundhog's Mirror: Reflecting on Change
The Weeping Angels' Christmas Curse
Burrowed in Time: A Groundhog Day Journey
Heartbeats: Poems to Share with Your Valentine
Dino Wicca: The Sacred Grimoire of Prehistoric Magick
Courage of the Pride: Finding Your Inner Roar
The Lion's Leap: Bold Moves for Big Results
Healthy Hustle: Achieving Without Overworking
Practical Manifesting: Turning Dreams into Reality in 2025
Jurassic Pharaohs: Unlocking the Magick of Ancient Egypt and Dino Wicca
The Happiness Equation: Small Changes for Big Joy
The Confidence Compass: Finding Your Inner Strength
Whispers in the Hollow: Tales of the Forgotten Beasts
Echoes from the Hollow: The Return of Forgotten Beasts
The Hollow Ascendant: The Rise of the Forgotten Beasts
The Relationship Reset: Building Better Connections
Mastering the Morning: How to Win the Day Before 8 AM
The Shadow's Dance: Groundhog Day Symbolism
Cupid's Kitchen: Quick Valentine's Day Recipes
Valentine's Day on a Budget: Love Without Breaking the Bank
Astrocraft: Aligning the Stars in the World of Minecraft
Forecasting Life: Groundhog Day Reflections

Bleeding Hearts: Twisted Tales of Valentine's Terror

Herbal Smoke Revolution: The Ultimate Guide to Nature's Cigarette Alternative

Winter's Wrath: The Complete Survival Blueprint for Extreme Freezes.

The Groundhog's Shadow: A Tale of Seasons
Burrowed Insights: Wisdom from the Groundhog
Sensual Strings: The Art of Erotic Bondage
Whispered Flames: Unlocking the Power of Fire Play
Forgotten Shadows: A Guide to Cryptids Lost to Time
Six Weeks of Secrets: Groundhog Day's Hidden Messages
Shadows and Cycles: Groundhog Day Reflections
The Art of Love Letters: Crafting the Perfect Message
Romantic Getaways at Home: Turning Your Space into Paradise
Purrfect Brews: A Cat Lover's Guide to Coffee and Companionship
The Groundhog's Wisdom: Timeless Lessons for Modern Life
The Shadow Oracle: Groundhog Day as a Predictor
Emerging from the Burrow: A Journey of Renewal
The Language of Love: Learning Your Partner's Love Style
Authorpreneur: The Ultimate Blueprint for Writing, Publishing, and Thriving as an Author
Weathering the Seasons: Groundhog Day Perspectives
Valentine's Day Magic: A Guide to Romantic Rituals
The Shadow Chronicles: Stories of Groundhog Day
Love and Laughter: Fun Games for Valentine's Day
AstroRealty: Unlocking the Stars for Property Success
The Groundhog's Path: A Guide to Seasonal Balance
Groundhog Day Diaries: Reflections in the Shadow
The Groundhog's Light: Illuminating the Path Ahead
Valentine's Traditions from Around the World
AI Wealth Revolution: Unlocking the Trillionaire Mindset
Love Rekindled: Reigniting Passion in Relationships
Single and Thriving: Self-Love on Valentine's Day
Emerald Legends: Mystical Tales of Ireland
Green Alchemy: Harnessing Nature's Magic
The Hearts of Horror: A Valentine's Day Nightmare

The Leprechaun's Guide to Wealth and Wisdom
Dancing with the Sidhe: Celebrating the Otherworld
Shamrocks and Shadows: Mysteries of the Green Isle
Emerald Energy: Harnessing Luck and Growth
The Gingerbread Golem's Valentine: A Sweetheart's Guide to Love and Enchantment
The Celtic Knot: Weaving Life and Destiny
Green Fire: Elemental Magic for St. Patrick's Day
Clover Chronicles: Finding Your Inner Luck
Ireland's Mystical Creatures: A Field Guide
Gingerbread Golem's Love Almanac
Prowl and Thrive: The Lion's Guide to Success
Love Alchemy: Transforming Your Life Through Heart Energy
WORLD DOMINATION: Woman's Rule 3:The New Life
The Midnight Rose: A Guide to Lunar Love Spells
The Forbidden Letters: Writing Your Own Love Prophecy
Luck and Lore: St. Patrick's Day for Modern Mystics
The Green Path: A Pagan Celebration of Renewal
The Dark Architect's Guide to Reprogramming Reality
Prankster's Paradise: A Guide to Harmless Hijinks
Manifest Your Reality: The Law of Attraction Simplified
The TARDIS Owner's Manual: Understanding the Doctor's Ship: *A complete guide to the TARDIS, its technology, secrets, and mysteries*
Starlit Romance: Astrology Secrets for Finding True Love
The Time Lord's Atlas: A Complete Guide to the Whoniverse: ***A breakdown of the locations, planets, and dimensions explored in Doctor Who***
Sweetheart Shadows: The Dark Side of Love and Attraction
February Fire: Reigniting Passion in Every Area of Life
The Self-Love Toolkit: 5 Ways to Embrace Who You Are
February Sparks: Ignite Your Dreams in 28 Days

March to Success: A 31-Day Action Blueprint
Ancient Paths: The 13 Sacred Principles of Dino Wicca
Echoes of Tomorrow: Navigating the AI Revolution
The Wellness Blueprint: Balancing Mind, Body, and Soul
Green Horizons: Sustainable Living for a Better Tomorrow
The AI Wealth Code: How to Make Millions with Automation
AI-Powered Creativity: Writing, Art, and Music for Profit
Extinction Rites: Rebirthing Your Soul Through Prehistoric Magick
Sacred Serpents tarot
Celestial Enchantment blank journal
Star Strains
Culinary Journeys: Exploring Global Flavors at Home
The Hollowvale Curse
The Hollowvale Harvest
The Egg of Transformation: Awakening Your Inner Power
Blooming Into Power: A Wiccan Guide to Spring Awakening
The Nightmare Nexus: The Third Doctor's Perilous Haunting
Digital Detox: Reclaiming Your Life in a Connected World
Ostara's Path: Walking the Spiral of Renewal
The Sacred Hare
Financial Freedom: Building Wealth in the Modern Age
Spring's Cauldron: Stirring the Waters of Change
The Hollowvale Pact
Quantum Consciousness: The Science of Reality Shifting
The Hollowvale Hunger
The Sacred Waters Within: A Witch's Guide to Hydrocephalus Magick
The Raven's Nest: Building a Life of Unshakable Stability
AI and the Human Mind: The Future of Intelligence
The Hollowvale Reckoning
Timeless Love: Building and Maintaining Lasting Relationships

The Raven's Roar: Unlocking Unstoppable Confidence
Raven Sight: Awakening Intuition and Inner Wisdom
The Butterfly Effect: Small Changes, Big Transformations
Taming the Boogeyman: How to Conquer Your Inner Fears
The Magick of Green: Awakening Earth's Energy in You
The Entrepreneurial Mindset: Secrets to Business Success
The Hollowvale End
The Shadow Luck Ritual: Reclaiming Power from Your Dark Side
Spring Magick for Beginners: A Simple Guide to Seasonal Energy Work
Doctor Who: The Hollowvale Conundrum
The March of Miracles: Unlocking Synchronicities in Spring
Unveiling the Cosmos: A Guide to Stargazing and Space Exploration
The Ultimate Guide to Surviving an Economic Collapse
The AI Gold Rush: How to Profit from the AI Revolution
Bastet's Shadow: The Hidden Power of Feline Magick
The Bastet Codex: Unlocking the Goddess's Magickal Secrets
Purring Spells: Harnessing Bastet's Healing Frequencies
Bastet's Nine Lives: Rebirth, Transformation, and Immortality Spells
Primal Currents: Hydrocephalus Magick in the Path of Dino Wicca
The Digital Gold Rush: Mastering E-Commerce and Online Sales
Future Shock: Adapting to the Next Decade of Change
The Quantum Mindset: Think Like a Billionaire
Sacred Motherhood: Awakening the Divine Feminine Within
The Mother's Spellbook: Enchantments for Love, Protection, and Prosperity
The Witch's Guide to Parenting: Raising Empowered and Intuitive Children

The Magick of Motherhood: Reclaiming Your Power Through Rituals
The Pagan Path to Self-Love: A Goddess's Guide to Worth and Confidence
Wild Woman Magick: Unleashing Your Primal Power
The Money Magnet Blueprint: Unlocking Unlimited Wealth
Biohacking 101: Unlock Your Body's Full Potential
The Wild Father: A Pagan Guide to Strength and Wisdom
The Sacred Masculine: Unlocking Your Inner Power
The Druid's Compass
The Warrior's Mindset
The Father's Fire
Odin's Path
Ancestral Bonds
The House That Whispers
The Magician's Code
The Wild Hunt
The Green Man's Path
The Altar of Success
The Shadow and the Sword
The High Priestess's Guide to Energy Healing
The Lunar Mother
The Sacred Self-Care Grimoire
The Womb Wisdom Codex
The Wheel of the Mother
The Witch's Guide to Manifestation
The Q2 Reset
The Ultimate Guide to AI-Powered Passive Income
Escape the 9-5
AI Feline Fortunes
The Tear-Stained Grimoire
Razorblade Runes
Cemetery Sirens

The Midnight Wristwatch
The Town That Forgets
AI Horror & Creepypasta
The Hollow Frequency
The Breach Echo
The Quiet Between Worlds
The Sigil of Tharan-Khul
Summon the Vault of Y'ha'ten
The Becoming Codex
The Profit of Az'ra-nar
The Drowned Logos
Echoes of the Eldritch Will
The Deep Ledger
Necronomicon of Networth
Covenant of the Wealthwyrm
The Whisperer's Manifesto
The Rites of Azh-K'luth
The Ark of the Crawling Coin
The Tithe of Shadows
Inkheart Abyss
The Timewinds of Y'ha-nthlei
The Spiral Labyrinth of Azag-Nirrh
The Gallifreyan Heresy of the Black Pharaoh
The Psalms of Nyog-Sotha
Black Rain Alchemy
The Infinite Maw
The Entropic Blueprint
The Oracle of Sh'guul
The Book of Breach
The Drowned Saint's Testament
Dreamcraft of the Sleeper God
The Silence Market
Cthonomics: The Dark Wealth Algorithm

Invocation of the Ten-Eyed King
Wealthbound to the Wyrm Below
Become the Unnameable
Codex of the Sovereign Flame
Rituals of Relentless Becoming
The Shadow Ascends
The Eyes Beneath You
The Will That Wakes Worlds
Silence Is a Weapon
The Mirror That Screams
The Whisper Between Moments
The Mind That Devours Fear
The Myth of the Finished Self
The Architect of Your Madness
The Voice You've Buried
The Discipline of Madness
Stormborn: Awakening Your Inner Tempest
The Mind That Ate Time
Unbind Your Becoming
The Pact You Owe Yourself
The Devourer's Diet
The Acid That Carves the Path
The Tower You Must Burn
The Breath Between Worlds
Speak Like the Deep
The Labyrinth Within
The Spine of the Sea God
Rejection Is a Portal
The Crown You Refused
The Scar Is the Spell
The Lightless Flame
The Habit of Becoming Horrific
ChickenJockey Chaos

The Gatekeeper Within
You Are Not Your Name
The Compass of the Mad
The Archive of Unsent Letters
What the Mirror Can't Show You
The Knife You Needed
Worship Nothing, Become Everything
The Other Voice
The Body the World Forgot
The Vein of the Void
The Black Bone Codex
The Puzzle of the Hidden Self (Millennium Puzzle)
The Eye That Sees the Lie *(Millennium Eye)*
The Ring of Return (Millennium Ring)
The Rod of Relentless Will *(Millennium Rod)*
The Tally of the Soul (Millennium Tauk/Necklace)
The Key to the Locked Timeline (Millennium Key)
The Scale of Sacred Decisions (Millennium Scales)
Inferno Bites: The UnOfficial Minecraft Lava Cookbook
Rot in the Attic
Prana: The Hidden Force of Your Infinite Self
The Shadow Realm Within: Transforming Darkness Into Destiny
The Borderland Collapse
Claws of Protection: Bastet's Defensive Magick
Mr. Ring-a-Ding's Madness
Yugioh Astrology: Celestial Deckcraft and Duel Destiny (2026–2027 Edition)
The Seal You Signed: Unlocking the Power You Once Feared
The Puzzle of Infinite Minds: Unlocking the Mentalism Hidden Within
The Eye That Mirrors the All: Secrets of Inner Reflection
Doctor Who: The Toymaker's Broadcast

The Rod of Eternal Flow: Commanding the Currents of Vibration
Golden Eyes of Bastet: Enhancing Psychic Vision
The Key of Dual Forces: Balance Within the Polarity
The Scales of Living Rhythm: Timing the Dance of Life
The Necklace of Hidden Cause: Weaving the Webs of Fate
The Ring of Secret Masters: Rising Through the All Within All
Daggers of the Dying Deep
Bastet's Wealth and Fortune Magick: Prosperity Rituals of the Goddess
The Tide that Speaks
The Scrolls of Petosiris: 13 Rituals from the Feathered Eye
Petosiris and the Living Plague of Osirion
Feline Fire: Bastet's Passion and Love Magick
The Star Altar of Petosiris
Bastet's Whiskers: Supernatural Sensory Magick
The Bastet Grimoire
Feeding the Shadows
The Mouthless Prayer
The Spiral Wound
Becoming the Ibis: Lessons from Petosiris's Mind
The Crimson Coven: Cola Magick for Sweet Dominion
Sacred Cat's Paw
The Soda Zodiac: A Flavor for Every Sign
Covenant of the Crawling Flame
The Ink of Ish'Zur
Frothroot: The Thirst That Ate the World
The Golden Glyphs of Prosperity
The Etherbind Codex
Echoes of the Resistance: Reclaiming the You That Survived
Harnessed Minds: Breaking Free from Mental Control
The Eyes in the Smoke

Rootwake: The Carbon Covenant
Skitter Logic: Unlearning the Fear That Built You
Doctor Who: The World That Froths
Rootwake: The Fizz That Rewrites Flesh
Rootwake: Frothfather of the World
The Holly Pact: Blood Beneath the Mistletoe
The 2nd Mass Principle: Building Unbreakable Tribes
Web of Wits: A Survival Guide to Encounters with Anasi the Spider (Aunt Nancy)
The Hexbreaking Handbook: Effective Spells to Remove Curses
Pop Alchemy: Transform Your Life One Sip at a Time
The Mason Code: Leading in Unleadable Times
Petosiris and the Fifth Chamber of Thoth
The Ether Seed Within
The Parent of Tomorrow
Petosiris's Pyramid of Perpetual Wealth
Unlearn the World
Grimoire of the Hollow Tongue
Zodiac Weeds: Finding Your Strain Through the Stars
Aquarius Rises in the Bank
The Sugar God's Smile
The Skinclock Reversal: Biohacking the Face of Time
Debtburn: How to Obliterate What You Owe Forever
The Ice Cream Oracle: What Your Cone Says About Your Future
Silence Is Sovereignty: The Power of Being Unreadable
The Wind That Whispers Through Stone
Path of the Four Directions
Doctor Who: The Maestro's Symphony of Endings
Oxygen Grail: Breathing to Undo the Clock
Zodiacal Collapse: When Stars Devour Time
Teachings from the Red Sand Silence

Doctor Who: Omega – The Broken Equation

Memory Wipe Your Past: Start Over Like a MiB

Mitochondria Prime: Ignite the Core of Youth

A Nest of Roaches

Grub from the Galaxy: MiB Recipes You'll Never Forget

Whiskers of Power: Bastet's Guide to Inner Sovereignty

The Gift Must Cost Them: Negotiation Through Unequal Exchange

The Worm Guys' Wealth Code: Hustle Like an Alien

Bug Out: The Edgar Method for Ruthless Goal Setting

Weaving Life with Spiderwoman's Pattern

Doctor Who: The Rani's Renaissance

How to Get a Job (If You're a Puppygirl)

Speak Through Others: The Art of Proxy Power

T-Rex Your Trauma: Reclaim the Power of Your Primal Self

The Black Briefcase: How MiB Stay Wealthy in Silence

The Thirst Beyond Reason: Understanding Diabetes Insipidus From the Inside Out

Backwoods Witchcraft for Billionaires: The Pagan Path from Dirt Roads to Gold Roads

The Moonshine Grimoire: Fermented Spells for Abundance

The Nameless Geometry

The Wraith's Mixtape: Spellcasting with Songs of Sorrow

The Gallifreyan Gentleman: Silent Wealth, Sonic Confidence, and the Doctor's Code of Living

Sugar Water Confidence

Dino Totems: Spirit Guides from Earth's First Gods

Pumpkin Sigils & Ritual Smoke

The Hózhó Compass

The Distortus Discipline – Order from Inner Mutation

Witchcraft for the Cold-Blooded Soul

Moonlight Over the Blessingway

Water, Interrupted: When the Body Forgets How to Hold On

Deformed but Divine: Embracing Your Asymmetry

Hexes in the Henhouse: The Farm Witch's Guide to Power

The Reversed Flame: A Grimoire of Inverted Power

Salt, Cells, and Sanity: Reclaiming Balance with Diabetes Insipidus

King of the Broken: Crowning the Flawed Self

Moonlight Scars: Emo Moon Magick and the Art of Lunar Sorrow

Noose Spells: Magick of the Hanging Rope

The Goth Cathedral: Rituals of the Broken and Beautiful

The Cretaceous Codex: Dino Spirits and Fossil Magick

The Turkey Bones Ritual

Nine Lives of Manifestation: Unlocking Bastet's Reality Codes

Chaos Muscles: Building Strength from Twisted Pain

Emo Blood Magick: The Veins of Power

The 3AM Flood: Nighttime Urination, Sleep Loss, and the DI Spiral

The Silence Between the Stars

The Lemon Method: Sour Your Way to Success

Starlit Sovereign

The Rite of Twelve Gates: Walking the Gates of the Duat.

Cornbread and Conjure: Recipes for Riches and Rootwork

The Black Rose Rituals: Emo Love Spells and Obsession Magick

The Eternal Goodbye: Death Magick and Rebirth Rituals

Sinkrot: The Drain That Remembers

The Hybrid Mindset: Thinking Beyond Evolution

Bone Dry: Navigating Dehydration Before It Breaks You

Wreathcraft: Winter Sigils and Yuletide Spells

The Rite of Twelve Mouths

S'mores of the Damned: Haunted Recipes for Halloween Night

Rethink the Drink: A Beverage Survival Guide for DI Warriors

The Shadow Chord: Guitar Magick and Sonic

Malformed Yet Majestic: Leading When You Feel Wrong Inside

The Cursed Diary: Ink-Stained Spells of the Emo Soul

Anxiety Off Switch: Emergency Reset for a Fried Nervous System

The Energy Heist: How to Take Back Your Life from Drainers

Beyond the Bathroom: Rebuilding Your Social Life With DI

Coyote's Gift for Decision Makers

Ghoul-Goo: Spooky S'mores You'll Die For

Echoes in the Mirror: Scrying and Self-Destruction Magick

Thread and Thorn: Stitching Spells from Rural Cloth

The Mogwai Mind: Building Untouchable Wealth from Small Ideas

Be Your Own Guide: Trust Your Inner Compass

Hormones in Chaos: The Endocrine Puzzle of Diabetes Insipidus

ChronoCleanse: Detox Your Biological Timeline

The Limb You Hide Is the One That Saves You

Leaves, Bones, and Whisper Spells

The Dinosaur Mindset: Prehistoric Tactics for Modern Wealth

Clawing Back Control: A Bastet Method for Boundaries and Empowerment

Samhain Codes of the Forgotten

Orange Alchemy: The Autumnal Spellbook

Monster Within, Master Without

The Sigil That Sleeps

Hearthcraft: Yule Hearth Sigils and Winter Warmth Spells

Temple of the Purring Moon: Rituals from Bastet's Lineage

When the Earth Remembers Your Footsteps

Food for Mood: Eat to Heal Depression, Not Just Survive It
Witch of the Kudzu Vine: Southern Pagan Wealth Secrets
The Invisible Diagnosis: Advocating for Yourself With DI
The Coffin's Lullaby: Sleep Magick and Nightmares as Portals
Ashes of the Will: Rituals for Erasing the Self
The Fracture Rite: Shattering the Magickal Core
Funeral Candles: The Art of Emo Flame Magick
The Black Grimoire: A Blank Ritual for Writing in Absence
Phantom Thirst: A Halloween Survival Guide for Diabetes Insipidus
The Hollow Crown: Emo Royalty and Magick of the Outcast King
Sandpainting for the Soul
Falling Into Balance: Using the Extra Hour to Recalibrate Life
100 Southern Superstitions That Still Work
The DI Child: A Parent's Guide to Raising Hydrated, Happy Kids
The Jungle of Shame: Escaping the Hidden Lab of Doubt
The Witch's Toast: S'mores Spells and Creepy Confections
The Hoodoo Pantry: Spells from the Mason Jar
The Immortal Fortune: Secret Wealth Lessons from Captain Jack Harkness
The Specter's Embrace: Magick for Channeling Ghostly Lovers
Grateful Waters: A Thanksgiving Survival Guide for Diabetes Insipidus
The Seizure Gospel
Harvestbind: Autumn Sigils and Samhain Spells
Doctor Who: The Algorithmic Awakening
Silent Nights, Steady Waters: A Christmas Survival Guide for Diabetes Insipidus
The Extra Hour Effect: How One Hour Can Transform Everything

Blade Between the Breaths

Running with the Mountain Shadows

Echoes of the Failed Experiment – Becoming a Living Legacy

Swamp Witches & River Ghosts: Real Southern Hauntings

Cornbread Prophecies: Magical Recipes from a Southern Table

Doctor Who: The Signal in the Star

Bloomcraft: Spring Sigils and Equinox Enchantments

Vanisher: How to Disappear from the Internet Without Losing Your Life

The Ultimate Christmas Cookie Cookbook

The Unbreakable Parent: How to Mentally Survive Raising Kids in a Broken World

Time Debt: How to Reclaim the Hours You Didn't Know You Lost

One Month, One Million: Unconventional Cash Creation Tactics

Doctor Who: The Cyber Conversion Protocol

Black Friday Frenzy: The Art of Finding Hidden Online Deals

The Grimoire Buried Under the Apple Tree

Digital Couponing Masterclass: Your Step-by-Step Guide to Black Friday Savings

The Fire Inside the Flint

Shadows on the Ceiling: The Emo Guide to Astral Magick

The Bone-Eaters Beneath Us

Black Friday Bundle Blueprint: Creating Irresistible Product Packages for Maximum Sales

Thirteen Nights of Unbinding

Doctor Who: Engines of Influence

Pumpkin Spice Alchemy: Recipes of Fire and Frost

When Raptor Met Rexy: Prehistoric Lessons in Wild Romance

Oblivion's Candle: Burn the Path Behind You

Campfire Curses and Chocolate: A Halloween S'mores Grimoire

The Wallet That Wasn't Mine: Breaking Free from Inherited Scarcity

The Cola Zodiac: What Your Fizz Says About Your Fate

Frostfire Fortune: Unlocking Winter's Hidden Prosperity

Signal Jamming: Detox Your Brain from Info Overload

The Dust of the Forgotten Rite

The Golden Cat Sigils: Drawing Power in Bastet's Name

Mud Magick: The Prosperity of Getting Dirty

Savory Spicefall: Beyond the Pumpkin Pie

Pumpkin Spice Apothecary Kitchen

The Pumpkin Spice Economy: Turning Trends into Billions

The Ember Veil: 13 Nights of Fire Magick

Financial Freeze: When Earning Triggers Panic

The Gingerbread Alchemist: Sweet Recipes with a Twist

Biosynth Power: Programming Yourself from Scratch

Echoes from the Talking Circle

Truffle Alchemy: Fungus of Fortune

Spores of Power: The Truffle Witch's Handbook

Doctor Who: The Tower That Speaks

The Mycelium Veil: Truffle Magick Unbound

Broke But Ashamed: Healing the Shame Wound of Debt

The Evergreen Mind: Growth Through Winter Stillness

The Black Veil Truffle Rite

The Voice Beneath Symbols

Witchlight on the Bayou: Swamp Spells for Sovereignty

I Grew Up Poor and Now I Sabotage My Success

The Lantern of Hollow Souls

Shutdown Survival: A Citizen's Guide to Thriving When Government Stops

When Abundance Feels Like a Threat: Healing the Hidden Fears of Enough

The Scarecrow Grimoire
Owls of the October Veil
Candlewax and Curses: A Halloween Spellbook
Excavating the Inner Fossil – Transforming Fossilized Thoughtforms into Tools of Power
The Yule Witch's Spellbook: Magick for the Holiday Season
Haunted Christmas: Ghost Stories for Winter Nights
The Christmas Survival Guide: Thriving Through the Chaos
The Bone Orchard Rites
Haunted Commerce: The Ghost in the Marketplace
When Money Triggers the Inner Child
Silent Night with the Silence: A Christmas Thriller
The Lightning Crown: Living and Leading Through Seizures
TARDIS Tidings: Festive Stories from the Whoniverse
Autumn Reset: Slowing Down Without Falling Behind
The Trillion Dollar Soul: Rewriting the Currency of Reality
Truffle Eclipse Magick
Micro-Manifestations: Quick Magick That Works
5-Minute Rituals for Busy Witches
The Marshmallow Massacre: Halloween Treats with a Sinister Twist
Blood and Blackberry Thorns
Magickal Mornings: Rituals for a Blessed Christmas Day
Embers of the All-Hallows Fire
The Pumpkin Market Collapse
The Hour You Gained: Transforming Time Into Power
The Chamber Must Be Sealed: Mastering the Power of Controlled Access
The Cursed Manuscript of Petosiris
The Festive Hearth: Creating Holiday Traditions
Darkness Rising: Thriving as Nights Grow Longer
Harvesting Time: Turning the Year's End Into Your New Beginning

Petosiris and the 13th Zodiac Key

Wagewound: When Paychecks Become Identity Prisons

Walls That Watch

The Silent Feast: Rituals of Power in the Longest Night

The Distortus Legacy : Becoming a Deformed King in a Perfect World

The Hollow Masks

The Gratitude Furnace: Forging Gold from Thanks

Feast of Inner Gold: Eating for Energy and Enlightenment

Haunted Commerce: The Season of Spending Spirits

Fear Bonds: How Panic Creates Profit

Black Friday E-Commerce Playbook: Sales Tactics to Skyrocket Your Holiday Revenue

Budgeting for Black Friday: A Holiday Savings Planner

Haunting the Harvest Moon

The Warrior's Water: Emergency Preparedness for People With DI

The First Sip of the Year: A New Year's Survival Guide for Diabetes Insipidus

Doctor Who: The Thirteenth Node

The Unseen Struggle: Mental Health, Anxiety, and Chronic Thirst

The Hearth's Hidden Ledger: Counting Energies as Currency

The Gift Alchemist: Turning Any Offering Into Gold

The Papyrus of the Bound Spirit

The Magick of Leftovers: Transmutation in the Fridge

Frost and Fortune: Christmas Wealthcraft for the Modern Magus

Last-Minute Gifts: Creative Ideas on a Budget

10 Secrets to Surviving Holiday Crowds

The Witch's Dow Jones

The Witches' Graveyard Shift

Pumpkin Sigils: Carving Rites for Midnight Power

The Secret Shopper's Black Friday Guide: How to Get Early Access and VIP Deals

Fever in the Foundation

The Neuralyzer Reset: Reprogram Your Morning Routine

Lightning Lessons of the White Painted Woman

The Enchanted Snowflake

The Magic Sip: Surviving Disney Parks with Diabetes Insipidus

The One Who Draws Through You

Santa's Secrets: A Magical Holiday Planner

Silent Bells, Loud Miracles: Self-Help for the Season of Stillness

The Sugar Spell Codex: Confectionary Magick of Christmas

Autumn Hexcraft: Fallen Leaves, Fallen Barriers

Sleep Like a Fortress: Build a Life Where Insomnia Can't Survive

Nowhere Was Ever Home

Christmas Under the Stars: A Celestial Holiday Guide

Rentproof: How to Never Be Evicted Again

Workless: Escape the 9-5 Without Being Broke

The Gilded Gift: A Wealth Altar for Christmas Morning

The Black Friday Grimoire

The Hollowing: Ceremonies of Spiritual Collapse

Doctor Who: The Nameless Signal

Where the Eagle Hides His Courage

The Dwarf Tyrant's Ascent: Claiming Power in a World of Giants

The Currency of the Dead: Trading with Spectral Bankers

The Icebound Witch: Survival and Magick in the Cold

The Emergency Money Mind: Constant Crisis, Zero Calm

Thirst & Roses: A Valentine's Survival Guide for Diabetes Insipidus

Springing Into Clarity: Mastering the Energy Shift of Daylight Saving

Speed of the Nanotyrant: Agile Strategies for Life's Hunt

The 90-Day Reset: A Science-Backed Guide to Reinvent Yourself Before the New Year

The Coil of Thorns

Timegates Unleashed

Dopamine Fasting 2.0: Rewiring Your Brain in a World of Overstimulation

The Nanotyrannus Mutation: Embracing Your Differentiated Form

Unwritten January: How to Use the Blank Page of the Year to Re-Author Your Life

Feast of the Forgotten Spirits: Ancestor Magick for the Holidays

The Burnout Codex: A System for Thriving Beyond Stress

I Don't Deserve to Have Money

When the King Doesn't See You: The Shadow Predator's Guide

The Reset Ritual :A Guide to Shedding Last Year's Weight—Emotional and Physical—by Spring Cleaning Your Soul

Calendar Alchemy: Learn to Bend Time and Productivity around Your Natural Rhythms

The Mirror Contract: A One-Sentence Agreement with Yourself that Unlocks Real Change

The Nile Formula: Sacred Flow for Millionaire Minds

Forward Momentum: Productivity Rituals for the Lost Hour

Harvest Gold: Wealth Magick of Pumpkin Spice Commerce

The Magick of Christmas Lights: Illuminating Holiday Rituals

Cranberry Crown: Royal Self-Worth through Ritual Meals

Petosiris and the Worms of the Feathered Throne

The Evergreen Equation: Self-Help for Sustained Growth

The Rain Will Wash Us Away: Emo Weather Magick
Snowlight Shadows: Magick Under Frozen Stars
Doctor Who: Merger of Empires
The Light Within the Feast: Magickal Wealth of Yuletide Flame
Momentum Machines: Small Habits Designed to Snowball into Unstoppable Forward Motion
Calm Spells: Magickal Solutions for Anxiety Relief
Santa's Final List: The Naughty Never Leave
The Mystic's Guide to Banishing Worry
The Silence Dividend: Turning Quiet Mornings into Compounding Growth All Year
Charmed Stillness: Rituals to Ease the Mind
Blood Spiral Ascension
The Vanishing Heart Invocation
Crystal Calm: Harnessing Stones for Anxiety
The Nano Tyrant Code: Strength in the Small Predator
The Energy Ledger: Accounting Methods for Vitality, Not Just Money
Snowglobe Mindset: Shake Up Your Thoughts, Settle Into Peace
The Weight of the Feather: Anubis's Codes for Soul Balance
Pocket Peppermint Power: Tiny Rituals for Big Holiday Energy
Shadowkeeper of the Golden Jackal: Anubis's Path to Energetic Protection
The Witch's Breath: Anxiety Relief Through Magickal Breathing
The Tiny Ember: Pocket Motivation for Cold Days
Stocking Sorcery: Mini Spells for Holiday Luck and Prosperity
Warm Hands, Steady Heart: Micro Grounding for Winter Anxiety

The Jackal's Lantern: Guide-Lights for Walking the Dark Path

Anubis's Silent Steps: Rituals for Stealth, Peace & Emotional Quiet

The Bonewake Protocol

Extinction-Proof: How to Outlive Trends, Trauma, and Time

The Fourth Doctor: The Eccentric Wanderer

The Second Doctor: Chaos and Charm in the TARDIS (Patrick Troughton, 1966–1969)

The Third Doctor: Earthbound Defender of Time (Jon Pertwee, 1970–1974)

The First Doctor: Genesis of the Time Lord (William Hartnell, 1963–1966)

The Fourth Doctor: The Eccentric Wanderer ***(Tom Baker, 1974–1981)***

The Fifth Doctor: Elegance and Empathy (Peter Davison, 1982–1984)

The Sixth Doctor: A Kaleidoscope of Conflict (Colin Baker, 1984–1986)

The Seventh Doctor: The Strategist of Shadows (Sylvester McCoy, 1987–1989)

The Eighth Doctor: A Time Lord's Renaissance (Paul McGann, 1996)

The War Doctor: A Time Lord's Burden (John Hurt, 2013)

The Ninth Doctor: The Healer of Worlds
(Christopher Eccleston, 2005)

The Tenth Doctor: The Lonely Hero (David Tennant, 2005–2010)

The Eleventh Doctor: The Madman in a Box (Matt Smith, 2010–2013)

The Twelfth Doctor: The Rebel with a Cause (Peter Capaldi, 2013–2017)

The Thirteenth Doctor: Breaking the Mold
(Jodie Whittaker, 2017–2022)

The Fourteenth Doctor: A New Beginning (David Tennant, 2022–2023)

The Fifteenth Doctor: Rewriting the Stars
(Ncuti Gatwa, 2023–2025)

Santa's Shortcut to Success: Micro Habits for a Better New Year

The Midnight Cocoa Manifesto: Comfort Rituals for Hard Nights

Why I Can't Save: Trauma Blocks to Financial Planning

Dino Brain, Mega Goals: Rewire Yourself for Savage Success.

Jurassic Profit: Unearth Your Inner Millionaire Fossil

Scales & Softness: Dating with Dino Heart

Carnotaurus Dreams.

Red Willow Thinking.

Reindeer Resilience: How to Keep Going When You're Exhausted

Candlewick Courage: Lighting Strength in Dark Seasons.

Elf-Mode Focus: Fast Attention Fixes for Busy Seasons

Futureproof Feelings: Emotional Skill-Building for Resilience No Matter What the New Year Brings

The 90-Day Rewire: Transform Your Neural Pathways Before Spring Blooms

Jolly Rich: Christmas Micro-Money Magick for Fast Prosperity.

Gingerbread Gratitude: Mini Practices for a Happier Holiday

Trauma-Spending: When Money Becomes a Drug

Goal Skeletons: Build Minimalist Frameworks for Resolutions That Last

The Snarl Strategy: Growling Back at a World That Silenced You

The Hourglass Reset: Reclaiming What the Clock Took

Yule Claw: Dino Rites of Light in the Darkness

Sacred Circles: Grounding Rituals for Anxious Souls

Clockstopper's Gut: Rebuilding the Core of Time

Winterfire Drive: Harness the Cold Season's Stillness to Ignite Deep Motivation

The 5-Minute Productivity Hack: Small Steps to Big Results

Light Ascending: A Self-Help Guide to Longer Days

Inner Economy: Trade Self-Doubt for Confidence Like a High-Value Currency

Simple Success: Decluttering Your Life for Better Results

The Resilient Mind: Thriving in Tough Times

The 2026 Playbook: Mastering the Year Ahead

The Spring Sleep Solution: Conquering Fatigue After Time Change.

The Hormonal Compass: Navigate Back to Your Youth

Golden Vision: Eating for Your Eye Color with the Power of Ghee

Lionhearted Love: Strength in Relationships

MiB Mindset: Think Like a Cosmic Agent

The Ladder of Small Wins: Climb Out of Stagnation by Stacking Micro-Victories

The Momentum Hour: Gaining More in Less Time.

The Year of You: A Self-Help Blueprint for Unapologetic Self-Ownership

The Dust That Watches You Back.

The Astral Parent

Shadow of the King: The Nanotyrannus Parable

Tiny Tidings of Triumph: Small Wins That Change Your Life

Dwarf Tyrant Rising: When You're the One They Overlook

The Bank Account Mirror: Healing How You See Yourself Through Money

Cretaceous Black

When Love Costs Too Much: Romantic Triggers and Financial Wounds

Dream-Eater's Guide to Wealth

Unzipped Reality: The Jacket That Opens Portals

The Power of No: How to Set Boundaries and Get Rich

Keeper of the Desert Veil: Anubis's Teachings on Illusion & Truth

Redacted Stargates: Stories the SGC Buried

The Clock That Dripped Time

Doctor Who: The Silent Acquisition

Hairline Manifestation: Unlocking Power at the Edge of Thought

Cash-Eater Crickets: How Insects Predict Economic Collapse

Dead Pet Whisperer: Grief Alchemy from the Other Side

The Love Algorithm Is Broken: Hack Romance Before It Hacks You

The Rite of the 8-Limbed Seal

Melt the Moon: A Fire Ritual to Reshape Emotion

Venomous Miracles: Healing Through the Poison Path

Wealth Without Water: The Post-Aquatic Rich Life

The Butterfly Betrayal: When Change Turns on You

The Quiet Upgrade: How Humans Are Secretly Rebuilding Themselves Without Asking Permission

Nobody Taught Us This: The Missing Human Manual for Money, Energy, and Self-Respect

You Were Never Broken: Why Most People Are Reacting Normally to an Unstable World

After the Noise Ends: How Humans Reset When the World Finally Goes Quiet

The Month That Tells the Truth: Why January Reveals What the Rest of the Year Hides

Tremors Party Unleashed: The Ultimate Guide to a Graboids Birthday Bash

Cold Start Human: Rebooting Motivation Without Forcing Momentum

The Year that doesn't start until they say

Love Without Performance: What Connection Looks Like When No One Is Watching

February Is a Mirror: What Love Exposes About You

How We Learned Love Wrong: Uninstalling Cultural Myths About Connection

You Are Not Too Much: Why Needing Love Is Not a Flaw

The Crooked Fence Covenant: Backwoods Boundaries and Witch Wealth

The Day That Keeps Repeating: Why Your Life Feels Stuck—and How to Shift It Gently

Nothing Changes Until Something Softens: Escaping Repetition Without Violence to Yourself

Same Life, Different Ending: How Tiny Choices Rewrite Repetition

The Loop Isn't Punishment: Why You're Being Asked to Learn, Not Suffer

Panic at the Register: Retail Anxiety and Public Shame

The Secret Formula to Becoming an Influencer in 90 Days

The New Rich: How to Retire by 35

Digital Nomad Secrets: How to Travel the World and Make Millions

Burn Your Waiting Room: Escape the Delay Spiral

Strapped for Pleasure: A Complete Guide to Pegging and Strap-On Play

Locked in Desire: A Guide to Chastity Play and Intimate Control

Burrowing into History: Groundhog Day Through the Ages

The Shadow Forecast: The Science of Groundhog Day

Choice Cascades: How One Decision in January Sets Ripples for the Whole Year

The Anti-Anxiety Blueprint: Mastering Fear and Stress for Success

The Ancestral Path of the Jackal Priest

Winterborn Titans: Giants of Ice and Stone

The Extinction Spire

The Emotion That Made Me Millions

Delete Their Voice: Become Unreachable

The Frostbound Mysteries: Mythical Beings of January's Chill

The Roar Within: Unlocking Your Potential

From Burrow to Sky: Groundhog Day Explained

The Boogey Book: Festive Ward-Off Edition

Fooled Ya! The Psychology Behind Great Pranks

April Fools' Alchemy: Transforming Everyday Items into Pranks

Anchor Habits: Root Yourself in Unshakable Routines That Endure Seasonal Change

Emerald Waters: A St. Patrick's Day Survival Guide for Diabetes Insipidus

The Groundhog's Legacy: Myths, Legends, and Facts

Six Weeks of Mystery: The Truth Behind Groundhog Day

The Upgrade Mind: Tech-Like Patches and Updates for Your Mental Operating System

Moon Blood, Star Flesh: Embracing Your Hybrid Nature

Groundhog Lore and Legend: A Complete Guide

You Are the Lie They Can't Kill

Download a Different Reality

The Quiet Advantage: Winning Without Announcing Yourself

A Year of Gratitude: Unlocking Joy

Touch Grass: A Pagan Reset for a Burned-Out Digital World

Cold Start Wealth: Building Financial Power from a Standing Still Point

Astrology Without Fate: Using Cycles Without Surrendering Control

The Future is Remote: Work Less, Earn More, Live Anywhere

Harvest of Silence

The Algorithm Knows Your Name

April Fools' Day for Introverts

Soft Power Systems: Influence That Doesn't Exhaust You

Practical Magick for Real Life: Focus, Intent, and Follow-Through

January Is a Lie: Designing Momentum Without the Calendar

Universal Flow: Managing DI in High-Energy Theme Parks

Electric Allure: Exploring Erotic Electro-Play

The Masked Embrace: Exploring Sensory Deprivation

The Ultimate April Fools' Survival Guide

Splashproof Survival: Waterparks & Wave Pools with DI

Agile Predator, Still King: Crafting Your Speed in a World That Celebrates Size

The Shadow Feast: Groundhog Day's Sinister Side

The Bug's Business Model

Edge of Bliss: Mastering the Art of Tease and Denial

Midnight Alchemy: Rituals for Transformation Between the Old Year and the New

Punxsutawney Bloodlines: A Groundhog Day Horror

The Burrower: Groundhog Day's Darkest Secrets

Buried Alive: A Groundhog Day Horror Story

Blood Moon Markets: The Witch's Guide to Wealth Magick

The Groundhog's Shadow: What It Means for the World

Seasonal Shadows: The Groundhog Day Phenomenon

The Shadow's Curse: A Groundhog Day Horror Tale

Punxsutawney Revealed: A Guide to Groundhog Day

Safari Hydration: Zoo & Wildlife Park Survival for DI

The Foolproof Prank Planner

Latex Lust: Embracing Fetish Fashion is a sophisticated

Whip & Whisper: The Dynamics of Impact Play

The Shadow Burrow Chronicles: Horror Beneath the Ground

Frozen Shadows: A Groundhog Day Thriller

The Groundhog's Revenge: A February Nightmare

Burrow of the Damned
Everyday Enchantment: Magickal Practices for Modern Living
Budget Bliss: The Easy Path to Financial Freedom
Six More Weeks of Terror
The Oxygen Debt
The Ice Veil: Mystical Beasts of January's Shadows
Roots That Remember
Polar Myths: Creatures of the Icy Abyss
The Marginalia Covenant
AI and the Occult: Digital Spirits, Sigils, and Cyber-Witchcraft
Roleplay Realms: Crafting Fantasies and Scenes
The Last Clean River
Lover in the Shadows: A Groundhog Day Tale
Buried Hearts: A Groundhog Day Gothic Romance
Anubis Wept for Petosiris
The Lantern Knows Your Name
Rituals of the Last Shadow
The Bell That Rings for No One
Shadows of Love and Death
The Groundhog's Bride: A Dark Valentine's Tale
Frozen Kisses: A Horror Romance for Groundhog Day
The Creative Spark: Igniting Your Passion Projects
From Cub to King: A Journey of Transformation
Six Weeks to Midnight: A Groundhog Day Romance
Tide of the Unclean
Burrow of Desire: A Groundhog Day Paranormal Romance
The Shadow Magick Almanac: Harnessing Groundhog Day Energies
AI for Emo Influencers: Growing an Online Following Without the Anxiety
AI for the Melancholy Millionaire: Making Money Without Social Interaction

Winter's Grip: A Horror Romance Beneath the Frost
Shadowed Hearts: A Love Buried in Winter's Chill
The Shadow Lover: A Groundhog Day Gothic Love Story
Beneath the Burrow: A Groundhog Day Thriller
The Punxsutawney Conspiracy
The Crimson Pact: Emo Blood Oath Magick
The Shadows of Gallifrey: A Doctor Who Horror Collection
Whispers in the Vortex: Chilling Tales from the TARDIS
AI Ghostwriting for Emo Souls: How to Make Money Writing Without Trying
The Anti-Social Emo's Guide to AI-Powered Freelancing

www.ingramcontent.com/pod-product-compliance
Lightning Source LLC
LaVergne TN
LVHW022009200926
848481LV00007B/2310